Wendy Blanco Donaire

Principle of Legal Reasonableness

AF209943

Wendy Blanco Donaire

Principle of Legal Reasonableness

Constitutional, Regulatory and Interpretative Control Parameter

ScienciaScripts

Cover image: www.ingimage.com

This book is a translation from the original published under ISBN 978-620-3-03387-8.

Publisher:
Sciencia Scripts
is a trademark of
Dodo Books Indian Ocean Ltd. and OmniScriptum S.R.L publishing group

120 High Road, East Finchley, London, N2 9ED, United Kingdom
Str. Armeneasca 28/1, office 1, Chisinau MD-2012, Republic of Moldova, Europe
Managing Directors: Ieva Konstantinova, Victoria Ursu
info@omniscriptum.com

Printed at: see last page
ISBN: 978-620-3-20876-4

Principle of Legal Reasonability

Msc Wendy White Donaire

Content

INTRODUCTION

There is no discussion that law and norms constitute a fundamental tool for the ordering of social life, whose primary purpose is justice and the common good.

The idea of reasonableness implies an examination of the "reasons" for the law and those rules to be enforced in a country, the rationality of the means and ends, explaining what is the justifying factor of the legal system.

In other words, the validity of a rule cannot be limited to a simple formal control; a control of reasonability and proportionality is necessary on the content itself as well as its harmony with fundamental rights.

When the legislator sanctions a norm, when the judge dictates a sentence, or the administrator issues an administrative act, it is sought in all cases to generate the necessary means to achieve a desired end. In this process of normative creation or legal interpretation, there is generally more than one alternative to the same purpose. When the norm is reasonable, not only in itself, but also with respect to the entire legal system, only in this way can it be considered to be in accordance with the law and thus fair.

This principle avoids unconscious decision making, insofar as public rules, acts and actions must be based on criteria of equity.

---

[1] Sapag Mariano A. (2008) The Principle of Proportionality and Reasonability as a Constitutional Limit of the State: A Comparative Study. Di Kaion No. 17 Universidad de la Sabana. Colombia.

Thus, this book intends to analyze Legal Reasonability from its definition, origin and scope as a General Principle of Law, in turn, analyzing the normative basis of the concept and its elements and applications to legal reality.

A. Definition of Legal Reasonability
B.

The word "Reasonability" comes from the Latin *"rationabilis", an* adjective that means arranged, just, according to reason; he who thinks or works in a way that cannot be censored (Lépiz 2009).

It alludes to reason, reasoning or something rational. Indeed, since the law is a human order, it requires the use of reason: hence the idea that the law is a rational order and will be a human order to the extent that it is reasonable.

Linares (2002) explains that in the science of Reasonability Law it is presented when sufficient reason for a shared conduct is sought, and by Reasonability in the strict sense it is only understood the foundation of truth and justice.

In this way, an intimate and close relationship between reason, truth and justice can be glimpsed. The idea of Reasonability, in a broad sense, implies an examination of the reasons for the Law, examining the rationality of the means and ends of the Law (Sapag 2008).

Reasoning is a chain of propositions significantly linked to each other, it is a means through which knowledge is obtained. Knowledge gives people security in the foundations of their beliefs and decisions in the world (González 1996).

But generally speaking, a legal reasoning cannot be considered as correct or incorrect, but it depends on the concrete situation to be resolved and the criteria that the authority applies for its resolution, being that what it resolves of one form at a given time, can be resolved from another at a later time.

However, reason cannot be limited to common sense, but must take into account that there is a process of disciplined observation and choice between values that underlie the legal system (Vargas 1998).

Now it is common to hear in the doctrine not only the term Reasonability but also rationality.

According to González (1996), Legal Rationality consists of an association of propositions by virtue of which conclusions are established by the conjunction of that conclusion with other propositions called premises. The reasoning will be valid to the extent that it obeys the rules of formation and transformation of the propositions, and the meanings of those propositions will be true to the extent that they are adapted to the reality of things.

Rationality is the activity of establishing reasoning to the conclusions that are reached.

That is, known things from which the reasoning starts, or judgments given from which it passes to a new judgment constitute the antecedent; that thing that one tries to know, starting from what is already known, is called consequent. Finally, the connection between the antecedent and the consequent, namely, that which makes it possible to pass from the first to the second, or that which legitimizes the transit or discourse from the antecedent to the consequent, is called the consequence (Mans 1978).

Analysts define reasonableness as the degree of sociological legitimacy to arrive at a given decision, and reasonableness as the procedure; a formal logical judgment. The Reasonability of Law is given by the intersubjective acceptance of the rational, which is fulfilled among a nucleus of men capable of agreeing on a subject (Bazán and Madrid 1991).

The Law demands a rational basis since in itself it is a game between means and ends: the ultimate ends of the Law (justice, common good), the intermediate or mediate ends, and the same means used to achieve the end. Since the law is a human order, it is essential to resort to the "reasons" of the law in order to justify it.

Some people state that Reasonability and Rationality are unified on the same point: rationality manifests itself according to man's dignity, whose operative aspect is Human Rights, and reasonability lies in all members of the universal audience.

In fact, in the eighties it was common to find the rational and the rationable as synonyms. For example Dromi (1980) defines rationality as follows:

"One of the limits of the exercise of freedom of appreciation that discretionary power implies is that it be exercised rationally. It is a consequence of the principle that imposes on the administration a logical and consistent action. Irrationality and illogicality then appear as a lack of consequence and of a logical nexus between the different parts that make up the administrative act.

In this case, there would be illogicality due to a contradiction in the motivation or in the device of the act or due to a lack of correspondence between the motivation and the device".

Although the author defines the concept of rationality, it fits perfectly to the meaning of Reasonability, making it seem that both are the same.

Others, however, claim that these two concepts are different: the first are those logical ideas accepted by a community or society and the second by philosophy as something divine (Perelman 1984).

From the legal point of view, Reasonability aims at the search for sufficient reason for a conduct, which can be in essence when a norm is formed, it is based on a fact or as a handle of justice.

Reasonability operates as a criterion that allows to arrive at a fair solution within the Law, whether it is a normative solution, a solution in a contentious process, etc. This fair solution requires that it be humane, not violent, not arbitrary: somehow, according to certain reasons (Sapag 2008).

In other words, this Principle simply implies justice.

The problem of justice is the correspondence or not of the norm to the superior or final values that inspire a certain Juridical Order. To ask oneself if a norm is fair or unfair is equivalent to asking oneself if it is fit or not to realize those values. And also a matter between what it is and what it should be (Bobbio 1994).

However, this principle avoids unconscious decision making, insofar as public rules, acts and actions must be based on criteria of equity.

Beyond the technical juridical formulation, this principle is related to the idea of material justice, remaining throughout history not only in the juridical thought but also in the moral and philosophical one, echoing in a proverbial language.

Hauriou (1979) defined it as *"a taste for rational organization"*. It is intelligible to an observer, who is endowed with a rational organization and who, when in the position of fundamental laws governing a series of determined phenomena, deduces a certain number of consequences that generally find verification in facts.

The Colombian Constitutional Court, also on multiple occasions, has defined the principle of Reasonability as synonymous with justice and equity. For example, it will be cited as in Ruling No. 530/93, expressed the following with respect to this comparison or relationship given to both terms:

"Reasonability" refers to the fact that a judgment, reasoning or idea is in accordance with the prudence, justice or equity that apply to the specific case. That is, when an action or expression of an idea, judgment or reasoning is justified by its convenience or necessity. Rationality expresses the exercise of reason as the rule and measure of human acts".

Both concepts, as can be observed, are closely linked, hence they are used in many occasions as if they were exactly the same, since they are related to justice, equity, although as can be observed, rationality is rather a rule to reason properly or a set of rules, while Reasonability is a little more philosophical or attached to a Law as such.

> *"Reasonability acts as a justifying factor of the legal order. When the legislator sanctions a norm, when the judge dictates a sentence, or the administrator issues an administrative act, it is sought in all cases to generate the necessary means to achieve a desired end. In this process of normative creation or legal interpretation, there is usually more than one alternative to the same purpose. When the norm is reasonable, not only in itself, but also in relation to the entire legal system, only in this way can it be considered "legal" and thus, fair"* (Sapag 2008).

As it can be noticed, Reasonability has been so important in the development of the Legal Order that it is used as a necessary starting point before talking about Law or even Justice.

> *"The question of the reasonableness of a law, a judgment, an administrative act or any normative act has implications that are linked to the very notion of law and justice.*

Understanding the notion of Reasonability must start from two basic premises: The first is that the right is a fundamental tool for men to organize their social life. The second premise is that the law seeks to fulfill an end which, it can be said, is to achieve just relations among men: the achievement of justice and the common good" (Sapag 2008).

It is then, besides a principle, also a useful tool for doing law.

"The mere allusion to this quality is not sufficient, since it requires an argument that is so dispersed and difficult to control, that in fact it leaves its content almost to the simple intuition of the legal operator. In the end, the requirements of proportionality are elements of the reasonableness of a legal decision, which can be applied without special reference to a legal culture because they are apprehensible to the human intellect" (Sánchez 2007).

The Constitutional Chamber of Costa Rica has repeatedly stated that the law cannot and should not be irrational, since the means selected must have a real and substantial relationship to the objective being pursued.

From this perspective, technical rationality means a proportionality between means and ends; legal rationality implies a compliance with the Constitution in general and, in particular, with the Rights and Freedoms recognized and guaranteed therein and in the International Human Rights Instruments duly in force in the country; and, finally, Reasonableness regarding personal belongings implies that no other limitations or burdens may be imposed on those Rights that are reasonably derived from their nature, nor greater than those indispensable for them to function reasonably in society2.

By demanding the Reasonability of the legal system, the aim is to minimize arbitrariness, seeking harmony with other principles such as Fundamental Rights, which operate as principles (Sapag 2008).

Campos (2000) mentions that this indeterminate legal concept is clarified when one penetrates the essential core of each right, such core is the one that does not tolerate suppression or, in other words, it is that core that cannot be extinguished, altered, damaged, or frustrated. When the core is preserved, the limitation to the Law is Reasonable; when it is affected, there is arbitrariness and Unconstitutionality. This is not intended to petrify this tool, but rather to allow judges to sufficiently and correctly base their decisions and arrive at fairer solutions.

It is clear, then, that, for example, as regards the imposition of criminal sanctions, in the case of assumptions of Reasonableness, they must be adjusted to the damage or injury inferred to the legal good and the consequences thereof.

---

2 Res. N° 20110-6805 Constitutional Chamber of the Supreme Court of Justice. San José, at ten hours and thirty one minutes of May twenty seven of two thousand and eleven

11

The role of a Constitutional Court in these cases is reduced to establishing whether or not the challenged assumption conforms to the limits of reasonableness and proportionality of the penalties that every legislator has in a democracy. It is not up to the Constitutional Chamber, for example, to determine, in any way, the amount of the penalties, or the way in which they are to be adjusted to reasonable parameters, but it can only indicate when the latter have been exceeded. [3]

The idea of such an abstract construction Principle is to subordinate any action to a Reasonability parameter aimed at assessing the relevance of such provisions. The most common application will be that in which a measure of differentiation is ventilated (Sánchez 2003).

This will impose the need to evaluate in a casuistic way the conditions that inform the factual species and to determine, according to the conception that on Reasonability the most acceptable solution is handled or attached to the common sense.

At the end of the nineteenth century, this concept of reasonability was **elevated to an axiological resource that limits the action of the legislative body**. Since then, we can speak of due process as a generic guarantee of freedom, that is, as a substantive guarantee. The overcoming of "due process" as a procedural guarantee is basically due to the fact that **the law, which has been adjusted to the established procedure and is valid and effective, can also harm the right**

[3] Res. n° 2008-05179 Constitutional Chamber of the Supreme Court of Justice. San Jose, at eleven hours of April 4, two thousand eight

_of_ the Constitution. In order to judge the **_reasonableness of the_** American doctrine, it invites us to examine, first of all, the so-called **_"reasonableness technique"_** within which the specific standard is examined (law, regulation, etc.) Once it has been established that the chosen standard is adequate to regulate a certain subject, it will be necessary to examine whether there is proportionality between the means chosen and the end sought. Once the criterion of " *technical reasonableness*" **_"legal reasonableness" must be_** analyzed.

In vote No. 5236-99 the Constitutional Chamber of the Supreme Court of Justice established the following components of Reasonability:

"To this end, this doctrine proposes to examine: a) Weighing reasonableness, which is a type of legal assessment that is applied when, in view of the existence of a specific precedent (e.g., income), a specific benefit is required (e.g., a certain amount of money). b) Reasonability of equality, which is the type of legal assessment that assumes that there must be equal consequences in the face of equal antecedents, without arbitrary exceptions; c) Reasonability of purpose: at this point, it is assessed whether the objective to be achieved does not offend the purposes set forth in the Constitution".

To this end, this doctrine proposes to examine: a*) pondering reasonableness*, which is a type of legal assessment that is used when a certain benefit (e.g. income) is required, and in this case it must be established whether it is equivalent or proportionate; b) the *reasonableness* of *equality is* the type of legal assessment that apart from the fact that in the face of equal precedents there should be equal consequences, without arbitrary exceptions; c) *reasonableness in the end*: at this point it is evaluated whether the

objective to be achieved, does not offend the purposes set out in the constitution. Within this same analysis, it is not enough to state that a means is reasonably adequate an end; it is also necessary to verify the nature and size of the limitation that a personal right must bear by that means.

Thus, if the same end can be reached by seeking another means that produces a less burdensome limitation on personal rights, the means chosen is not reasonable. It was in the sentence number 01739-92, of the eleven hours forty-five minutes of the first of July of nineteen hundred and ninety-two, where for the first time an attempt was made to define this principle, in the following way:

*"**Reasonableness as a parameter of constitutional interpretation** ... but which among us, especially in the absence of that need, **would simply be equivalent to the principle of reasonableness of laws and other public or even private rules or acts as a requirement of their own constitutional validity, in the sense that they must be adjusted, not only the rules or***

concrete precepts of the Constitution, but also to the sense of Justice

which implies, in turn, the fulfillment of requirements

equity, proportionality and reasonableness, understood

These as suitability for the purposes proposed, the principles

assumptions and values presupposed in the Law of the Constitution. *From there that the laws and in general the norms and acts of authority require for their validity, not only to have been promulgated by competent organs and due procedures, **but also to pass the fundamental revision for their concordance with the norms, principles and supreme values of the Constitution (formal and material), such as those of order, peace, security, justice, freedom, etc., which are configured as patterns of reasonableness. In other words, a public or private norm or act is only valid when, in addition to its formal conformity with the Constitution, it is reasonably founded and justified in accordance with constitutional ideology. This ensures not only that the law is not irrational, arbitrary, or capricious, but also that the means selected have a real and substantial relationship to its purpose. A distinction is then made between technical reasonableness, which is, as stated, the proportionality between means and ends; legal reasonableness, or compliance with the Constitution in general, and especially with the rights and freedoms recognized or assumed by it; and finally, reasonableness of the effects on personal rights, in the sense of not imposing on those rights other limitations or burdens than those reasonably derived from the nature and regime of***

rights themselves, nor greater than those indispensable for their reasonable
functioning in the life of society.

Legitimacy, then, refers to the fact that the objective sought with the act or provision challenged must not be, at least legally, prohibited; suitability indicates that the state measure challenged must be capable of effectively achieving the objective sought: Necessity means that, among several measures that are equally suitable for achieving that objective, the competent authority must choose the one that affects the individual's legal sphere as little as possible; and proportionality in the strict sense means that, apart from the requirement that the rule be suitable and necessary, the measure must not be out of proportion to the objective sought, that is, it must not be "enforceable" on the individual 5

C. Origin of the Principle of Reasonability

The principle of reasonableness has its roots both in Anglo-Saxon law *(due process of law)* and in European law (where it is called the principle of proportionality); its birth and development have occurred simultaneously, but with similar scopes in both traditions (Sapag 2008).

It was then tacitly mentioned by the jurisprudence of the Supreme Court of the United States of America, in the wake of the 14th Amendment to the Federal Constitution.

---

[4] Ruling number 01739-92, of eleven hours forty-five minutes of July 1, 1982, Constitutional Chamber of Costa Rica.
5 Judgment number 03933-98, dated June 12, 1998, at 9:59 a.m., Constitutional Chamber of Costa Rica.

This jurisprudence was directly focused with the Common Law, referring therefore to the development of the natural law and the value of justice.

When the natural law declined, positivism triumphed and the assessments themselves assumed the form of fundamental rights. The first reference to this principle dates from 1610, when Judge Edward Coke established that when an act of Parliament was contrary to common law and reason, it should prevail and such an act should be declared without value. This is where the principles of equality and due process come in.

The demand for due process evolves to be understood as a guarantee of respect for citizens' rights and not only procedural rights by the public authorities (Pereira 2004).

"In the initial conception 'due process' was directed to the procedural prosecution of the legislative act and its effect on substantive rights. At the end of the nineteenth century, it was elevated to an axiological resource that limits the action of the legislative body. Since then, we can speak of due process as a generic guarantee of freedom, that is, as a substantive guarantee. It is due to the fact that the law that has been adjusted to the established procedure and is valid and effective can also harm the right of the Constitution. In order to make the judgment of reasonableness, U.S. doctrine invites us to examine, first, what is known as technical reasonableness, within which the specific norm is examined.

In order to regulate certain matters, it will be necessary to examine whether there is proportionality between the means chosen and the end sought" (Constitutional Chamber of the Supreme Court of Justice of San José, Res. 20110-6805).

This principle of Reasonability or Proportionality is born.

Both in the United States through the evolution of Constitutional jurisprudence on the right to due process as well as in Europe in the search for legitimacy of the activity of public entities achieving the interdiction of arbitrariness resulting from the experiences of the first half of the twentieth century (Lépiz 2009).

These are criteria of jurisprudential creation, which were not initially included in any positive text. Thus, both on the basis of Continental European Proportionality and on the basis of Anglo-Saxon Reasonability, today national and international courts take into account the proportion between means and ends in order to decide on the respect of public acts for citizens' rights (Pereira 2004).

As for Costa Rica, there is no clear idea as to the origin and concept of the principle of reasonableness in the rulings of the country's Constitutional Chamber, nor is there any chronological or technical uniformity in the application of this principle.

Although what is known is that since the creation of the Constitutional Chamber in 1989, this concept has begun to be handled and applied, recognizing its value as an unnamed Constitutional Principle that integrates the parameter of the Constitutionality block (Vargas 1998).

It is therefore necessary to clarify that in countries such as Colombia, Mexico, Argentina and other European countries, such as Germany, Switzerland, Spain and France, among others, they use the concept of Reasonableness and they see it as Proportionality which, however, for the purposes of this study is exactly the same.

"The constitutional principle (of proportionality) by virtue of which public intervention must be "susceptible" of achieving the desired end, "necessary" or indispensable in the absence of another measure less restrictive of the sphere of freedom of citizens (that is, because it is the gentlest and most moderate of all possible means or law of minimum interventionism) and "proportional" in the strict sense, that is, "weighted" or balanced because it derives more benefits or advantages for the general interest than harm to other goods, values or goods in conflict, in particular rights and freedoms".

This principle is a jurisprudential criterion used in the Anglo-Saxon and continental law to judge the actions of both the public power and the individuals in relation to the rights of the citizens. And although they are usually considered to be comparable (Proportionality and Reasonability), however, both principles had different origins (Pereira 2004).

B.1 Origin Proportionality

The term Proportionality comes from the Latin *"proportionalitas- atis"* which means conformity or proportion of some parts with the whole or related things. Proportionality" denotes the conformity or due correspondence of the parts of a thing with the whole or among related things, implying the adverb "proportional", something regular, competent or suitable for what is necessary (Vargas 1998).

In the legal field, based on thinkers of Western tradition such as Pythagoras, Aristotle, Thomas Aquinas and others, he considers proportionality as a derivative of the principle of proportionality as a derivative of equality, and of justice.

The birth of the Principle of Proportionality is analyzed through the formulation of the separation of power as an institutional framework. It is the balance of powers that will help us to know where the judge controls and from where his discourse will have to be refined, if he does not want to lose legitimacy the reason that the Constitution entrusts to him (Fernandez 2008).

Among the juridical and political assumptions that determined its birth and formation, the conception of the Liberal State that emerges from the contemporary age, after the outbreak of the French Revolution at the end of the 18th century, and throughout the 19th century, stands out. The new Liberal State assumes the preservation of peace and security as the well-being of citizens. This principle is used for the first time specifically in Criminal Law.

In 1764, the first copy of the book *"De los Delitos y las Penas"* by Cesare Beccaria appeared in Europe, which denounced the atrocities of that time, due to the lack of proportionality between the crimes and the penalties, since torture and death penalty were common at that time, with a secret investigation, with no right to defense where the key was to confess the guilt at all costs (Vargas 1998)

It was precisely Beccaria (1968) who stated that penalties should be proportionate to each other, not only in terms of force but also in terms of how they are violated.

Montesquieu in his "Persian Letters" (1717) also mentioned this same principle as a requirement for punishment.

The first direct allusions to this in law texts are found in *"Carl Gottlieb Svarez"*, editor of the 1974 Prussian General State Law.

It emerges as a classic concept of criminal law known as the *"prohibition of excess" that* dates back to the jurisprudence of the High Court of Administrative Litigation of Prussia (1875-1941) (Sapag 2008).

But it was in the Declaration of the Rights of Man and of the Citizen (1789), after the French Revolution, that it was explicitly established.

Indeed, this principle is known in the Declaration of the Rights of Man and of the Citizen (1789), which proclaimed that the law should not establish other penalties than those strictly and evidently necessary. At the beginning of the 18th century, Jon Locke theorized about the constitutional monarchy, pointing out that *"the power of a free and reciprocal convention, between men, whose result is the State, institution that must protect property rights and equality before the law*" (Fernandez 2008).

The enlightened ideology whose most outstanding representatives are Hobbes, Locke, Montesquieu and Rousseau, emerges two cultural currents of the eighteenth century: first, rationalism, which replaces the principle of authority with logical reasoning as an instrument to know reality, and second, the scientific method.

This criterion in the Criminal Law consisted in the requirement that the penalties must be graduated in a manner that is proportional or reasonable to the crime; and that they be established with some degree of proportionality based on the social importance of the act and the legal asset protected (Sapag 2008).

Thus, after the French Revolution, in Germany, the first indication of this in relation to the criminal process took place in a resolution of the deutscher Journalistentag, taken in Bremen on August 22, 1875, which requested that coercive measures against journalists who refused to testify as witnesses be proportionate to the penalties established for the crimes being prosecuted (Vargas 1998).

It was in the nineteenth century, it moved from Criminal Law to Administrative Law and was coined as a criterion of control over the discretionary powers of the administration and as a limit to the exercise of police power.

Otto Mayer, founder of German Administrative Law (1982) explains that the measure of the police power requires that it be proportionate, which derives from the law and the very nature of the exercise of this power: it is a natural measure that *"acquires the importance of a serious legal limit"*.

Then from the eighteenth century, it is used to judge the activity of the executive branch, especially the police. The principle prohibits the excess of public action with respect to its purpose, and thus, as a prohibition of excess, it is enshrined in German law.

The German doctrine cites the Polizeirecht as the first legal-administrative treaty where this principle is formulated, which is also found in Mayer's work, for which the rule of proportionality functions as a natural measure of police power, acquiring the importance of a legal limit (Fernández 2008)

The German Federal Court quickly considered that the traditional principles of administrative law were constitutional principles, and thus took the maxim of proportionality to the control of state acts regulating or intervening on fundamental rights.

The Principle of Proportionality has now become a general administrative rule, with a required reference in every activity, provided that it can be carried out within a margin of appreciation and the legislator has not fixed the appropriate necessary and subsidiary measure that the administrative operator must adopt.

In Judgment No. 77, 179 of the First Chamber of the German Federal Constitutional Court of December 15, 1965, it mentions

"In the Federal Republic of Germany the principle has constitutional status. It originates in the principle of the rule of law, in the essence of fundamental rights, which as a general expression of the right of the citizen vis-à-vis the state, can only be limited in a broad way by the public authority, when this is indispensable".

Both the jurisprudence and the German Constitutional doctrine understand this principle as the maximum criterion delimiting the essential content of the Rights, and it is considered a primary institution of the German Constitutional Law. In fact, in the second post-war period, this concept would pass into the field of Constitutional Law, hand in hand with the German Federal Constitutional Court.

It must be proportionate to the evil it seeks to prevent, and the authority must choose those means that produce the least harm to the interests of individuals. The intervention must always be proportional to the circumstances.

The Spanish constitutional court has come to say that the area in which the principle of proportionality is normally and particularly applicable is that of fundamental rights.

In fact, in Ruling 66/1995 the Spanish Constitutional Court refers for the first time to this principle, effectively, as an examination of the constitutionality of interventions in fundamental rights. Since then, the principle of proportionality has been applied in case law as a structural criterion for determining the content of these rights (Alexy 2007).

European law receives this principle through case law and it is included in the consolidated version of the Treaty establishing the European Community and in the annexed Protocol on the application of the principles of subsidiarity and proportionality.

Indeed, the principle of proportionality is a principle that is now widely used in the field of constitutional justice and has acquired enormous weight in the jurisprudence of the European Court of Human Rights in Strasbourg and in the jurisprudence of the Court of Justice in Luxembourg. At the European level, the principle of proportionality has been explicitly enshrined in some constitutions and in the Charter of Fundamental Rights of the European Union. This principle must be understood as a criterion affecting the normative development of rights. The principle of proportionality, in the field of the theory of rights, is included within the generic issue of limits. The operationalization of the principle of proportionality necessarily implies the existence of limiting contents that can be extracted from the meaning of the norms, normally constitutional (de Assisi 2006).

Therefore, the European version of the principle of reasonableness has been understood as a tool to elucidate the essential content of fundamental rights in the face of a rule that regulates or restricts them, and constitutes, in turn, a criterion for the substantiation of judicial decisions that deal with them.

Today, the principle has experienced an extraordinary boom, and its use has been generated in almost all legal areas, particularly in the

Administrative Law in which it has become a fundamental guiding principle, which operates as a limit on that state activity that acts on the scope of freedom of citizens, and as an instrument in the material legal control of discretionary decisions (Fernandez 2008).

B.2 Reasonability as a Principle

Jurists have always known that the law cannot be understood, nor handled professionally, without resorting to principles that are usually not expressly formulated as such in the laws themselves or other official provisions.

For at least a hundred years, this has been the subject of reflection in studies on the subject, from the most generic to the most specific. Some of these examinations became well known, even internationally (Del Vecchio, Betti, Esser, Crisafulli, Spiro, Boulanger, Jeanneau, Wolf, Van der Meersch, Carrió, Garstka).

In Spain the Constitutional Court says that the Theory of Principles is a milestone (Ruling 66/1995).

The fact that there is a heterogeneity in the Principles allows them to be used, one or another, for more than one type of interpretative methodology, used by jurists. These are not only found within the framework of dogmatic methodologists, but can also claim a role as axiological, teleological or empirical sociological methods. Otherwise, they can be obtained in terms of voluntary psychological or realistic sociological methods or even grammatical literal ones (Haba and Barth 2004 p 24).

The Principle of Reasonability is a General Principle of Law. This means, that it enjoys juridicity: it is obligatory in the application of the Law in general.

The fact that it is considered as a Principle means that unlike rules that are norms that do not admit degrees, a Principle admits its application in degrees but demands its maximum possible compliance; they are *"optimization mandates"*, according to Alexy Robert's definition (1993).

Even this means that it is part of the legal system regardless of whether it is expressly declared or not. The status of principle gives it a degree of abstraction and indetermination; this is why it has been said that the Principle of Reasonability is an indeterminate legal concept.

Functionally, the Principles of Law, base and limit the Law, both supra positive and positive, from within the Law, insofar as they act with and through it. They are a consequence of natural law (Haba and Barth 2004).

Reasonability is then a factor that legitimizes the Law.

And as such, the controversy arises as to whether it is a rule of law or a principle of law, from which its distinction has been the cause of confusion and controversy with a variety of criteria for distinction.

The distinction between Principles and Rules: It constitutes the basis of the fundamental ius foundation and is a key to the solution of central problems of the dogma of Fundamental Rights.

When the difference between Rule and Principle is best perceived is at the moment of its application, or when the rules collide.

The Principle is not the same as a rule of law, since the regulated powers are characterized by the fact that the legal norms establish in which conditions the administration must act and how it must act. They define the only behavior of the Administration without any margin of subjective appreciation.

One of the most proposed criteria is that of generality, where the Principles are standards of a relatively high degree of generality, while the rules are of a relatively low level. Thus, for example, a Principle is the one that allows religious freedom, and a rule with low generality would be a law according to which every prisoner has the right to convert others.

Perhaps the distinction between principles and rules is to be conceived not in terms of the defeatability of the guidelines in question but in terms of the degree of openness or concreteness of the guidelines. Perhaps most legal guidelines are defeatable, although the degree of openness of their conditions of application determines that we speak of principles and rules (at least in some contexts): when there is a certain list of explicit conditions one tends to speak of rules, when the conditions of application are all implicit one tends to speak of principles. Be that as it may, we can adopt this stipulation and contemplate the collisions between principles or as problems of conflict between guidelines that establish duties or unconditional rights, *prima facie* (Fernandez 2008).

The decisive point for the distinction between Rules and Principles is that the Principles are rules that command that something be done as much as possible, within the existing legal and real possibilities.

Therefore, the Principles are mandates of optimization, which can be fulfilled to different degrees and the extent of their fulfillment depends not only on the actual but also on the legal possibilities.

Rules, on the other hand, are norms that can only be fulfilled or not. If a rule is valid, then exactly what it demands must be done, no more and no less. Therefore, rules contain determinations in the area of what is factually and legally possible.

Fernández (2008), for example, analyzed the Spanish legal system and showed that it has not enshrined the principle of reasonableness (proportionality in Spain) as a constitutional principle, but on the contrary, the times it has been used have been as a relative concept.

However, she goes on to explain how it is common to use unwritten General Principles of Rights to fill gaps in the law, including the principle of Proportionality or Reasonability, which in turn will also serve to limit and reduce the scope of the Legal Rules explicitly formulated in the Law.

It has been determined that the Principles of Reasonableness and Proportionality are Constitutional Principles, which, as already indicated, are a subcategory of the General Principles of Law and therefore fulfill the same functions of the latter, namely: that they are superior principles that

They inform the entire legal system, which they support and which constitute a means of interpreting the law.

However, in spite of its importance, a series of criticisms, mainly of a theoretical-methodological nature, have been made of the Principle. Among these criticisms is the accusation of lack of conceptual clarity, which its use triggers a justice that is difficult to control in the concrete case, the difficulty of identifying in strictly legal terms the Rights and goods that are used in its operation, the incommensurability, the impossibility of objectively measuring advantages and sacrifices in the dissatisfaction or satisfaction of the Rights (from Assisi 2006).

The criticisms of the principle of proportionality raise two questions of unquestionable significance. On the one hand, the accusation of lack of justification of an analysis of the Rights of Certainty existing in the use of this Principle. This criticism shows that the use of the Principle of Proportionality is something that is enormously valuable, that is, independently of whether it is carried out taking the constitutional text as a reference, it implies adopting questionable points of view, meanings, and hierarchies of values.

What can be assured, by way of synthesis, is that regardless of whether we speak of Reasonability as a Principle or a Rule, from both perspectives we speak of a norm, since both establish what is due (Alexy 2007).

So every rule is either a Rule or a Principle, so regardless of whether it is a Principle, its value is equivalent to a Rule.

D. Reasonability as Constitutional Control

The Principle of Reasonability is also the method usually used by the Courts to solve the circumstantial collision between Fundamental Rights or between Rights and other Constitutional goods.

It is an unnamed constitutional principle, which functions as a limit to the restriction of fundamental rights, and which must be respected by the legislator, the judge and the public administration (Vargas 1998).

The legal operator must seek to maximize Reasonability either in the sanctioning of any normative act, in the interpretation, in its application and control.

Since the regulated powers establish a single due course of action, they cannot be subjected to the scrutiny of the Principle of Reasonability which is aimed precisely at evaluating the choices made by the administration. There is no subjective judgment to be evaluated (Lépiz 2009).

The administration lacks freedom since it is obliged to strictly comply with what is established by law, without any loopholes to appreciate the facts and to make a choice. Hence, the regulated powers cannot become the object of Reasonability Control. This Principle was then conceived for a superior and more complex analysis: the Judgment of convenience and opportunity.

The legal term, which combines characteristic elements of the justice of the specific case, measures the impact on citizens of state intervention, of the logic, of moderation in the exercise of power; with the burden or duty to motivate that falls to the State (Fernández 2008).

The starting point is to analyze how the different legal systems have used criteria of control over the content of the laws and their conformity with the constitutional order. This control is known as the requirement of Reasonability of the laws. Since it is a maxim of the Law; that laws must keep a certain degree of Reasonability to be in conformity with the Constitution, this requirement has been raised to the level of a constitutional principle (Sapag 2008).

The idea with this is to value the legitimization of public action and that, in turn, legitimization is the prohibition of arbitrariness (Lépiz 2009).

"As is well known, the principles of reasonableness and proportionality are established in the social and democratic state of law as an insurmountable limit to arbitrariness. Hence, today the theory of interdiction of arbitrariness is peacefully accepted. For this reason, the exercise of discretionary powers does not authorize any organ or entity to issue rules and arbitrary acts that violate elementary principles of justice and equity. In this sense, the laws, as well as the acts of the Public Administration, must be suitable, necessary and proportional in the strict sense. On the other hand, it is a thesis of principle in the most authoritative doctrine of Constitutional Law and the Constitutional Courts, as well as the Courts

International Human Rights Law, the validity and application of these principles. Indeed, it has been clearly stated that Reasonableness is a constitutional principle, which derives from the rule of law as a guarantee for the protection of fundamental rights" (Constitutional Chamber of the Supreme Court of Justice San José Vote: 20110-6805. Res. 20110- 6805).

In Ruling No. T-260-93 of the Colombian Court, the following is indicated:

"This privilege of the administration, in the decision and execution of its acts, remains a privilege but it cannot be arbitrary because the administration is not an end in itself but is at the service of the community and because it is of the essence of the social state of law that the legal protection of the worker is executed, without delay. In other words, administrative self-guardianship has a limit: Reasonability".

Fernandez (2008) mentions that:

*"It combines characteristic elements of justice, measures the impact on citizens of state intervention, of the logic of moderation in the exercise of power, with the burden or duty to motivate that falls to the state. The raison d'être, then, of the prohibition of excess or proportionality **(Reasonability)** lies in the need to legitimize State action in order to prevent the citizen from becoming a mere object or recipient*

of public intervention. It is considered the oldest and most general legal control of state intervention" (Bold is not from the original).

There is a need to legitimize the state action and the measure of the instruments that can legally be used, in order to avoid that the citizen becomes an object and rather an individual with the certainty that the rules and measures that are applied are the most relevant.

It also operates as a constitutional limit to the power of the State, and a criterion for controlling the rules so that their content is in accordance with the law and that Fundamental Rights are not affected or altered (Sapag 2008).

It could be said that it is presented as a control by citizens over power through their representatives.

It is precisely within the Principle of Constitutional Supremacy that the Principle of Reasonability is located as a sub-principle, whose purpose will be a parameter for the evaluation of legal acts, whose requirement must be oriented to respect the values expressed in the constitution.

The jurisprudence of the Constitutional Chamber of Costa Rica mentions the following in relation to this matter:

"This power is subject to the principle of constitutional supremacy, which imposes the observance of the principle of reasonableness and proportionality, under which the provisions issued by the Legislator must be examined.

Likewise, the means used by the State to avoid the aforementioned conflict must not place the addressee in a situation that makes the enjoyment of his fundamental rights nugatory" (Constitutional Chamber, No. 1749 of 2:30 p.m., March 7, 2001).

The position of the Principle of Reasonability has been recognized as derived from the Principle of Constitutional Supremacy.

The analysis of the Constitutional validity of a norm cannot be limited to a mere formal or adjective control; a Constitutional Control of Reasonability and Proportionality is necessary on the very content of the norm: the arbitrated means and its ends, and its respect for Fundamental Rights (Sapag 2008).

In short, Reasonability marks a limit for public activity that, if exceeded, means a violation of the Political Constitution that must necessarily be corrected, either by expelling it from the system or by fixing it so that it conforms to the exercise of Fundamental Rights.

For its part, the Spanish Constitutional Court, in Ruling No. 55/1996 of March 28, 1996, referring to the principle of reasonableness, warned that in that Order it does not constitute an autonomous canon of constitutionality whose claim may be made in isolation from other constitutional precepts. It is, if you will, a principle that can be inferred from certain constitutional precepts and in particular from those invoked here and, as such, it operates essentially as a criterion for interpretation.

The Constitutional Control of Reasonability is not infallible since its results will depend, to a great extent, on the legal operator, and his assessment and interpretation of the facts, of the Constitutional Rights, his fundamental views, of the means used by the norm and the understanding of the end or aims of the same. The principle is that sentences should be based on clear and precise reasons and arguments in order to make decisions in one direction or another.

On the other hand, Otto Lépiz (2009) assures that Reasonability has a relative character and that it depends on the intrinsic circumstances of whoever has to resort to it, because it obeys their vision and experience of life.

However, not everything reasonable is always fair. History is full of examples of reasonable but inherently unfair measures. This is not to say that an argument solidly based on Reasonableness contributes to achieving justice.

E. Legal Reasonableness Fundamentals

The Constitutional Jurisprudence considers the Principle of Reasonability as one more of the integral principles of the Constitutional Law, which meets the requirements of generality and juridical potentiality. Although it is true that it is not expressly regulated by the Constitution, some articles present vestiges (not clear or sufficient to support a position) that may be considered (Sánchez 2003).

Since it is part of the Constitution, it is part of the legal system, of which it is the source and the principle of its formation.

Article 24 case on the obligation of officials to "reason" resolutions allowing the intervention of communications. On the other hand, there is Article 173, paragraph 1, regarding the reasoned veto in municipal matters. As indicated above, both articles are not the basis for the principle of reasonableness, but they do allow for the establishment, at least "literally," of a bias toward the consideration of this principle (Sánchez 2003).

Furthermore, Article 28 of the Political Constitution of Costa Rica, from which the Constitutional Principle is derived, states that the legislator is inhibited from regulating actions that are not contrary to moral public order or good customs. At the same time, the principle of reservation of law is obtained, that is, when a matter must be regulated solely by the legislator to the detriment of the competence of other branches or organs of the State.

Other authors derive the principle from a study of Articles 39 and 40 of the Political Constitution, which are interpreted with the principle of due process, concluding that they contain an antithesis to the constitutional ideology of any punishment imposed in a disproportionate manner, such as inhumane punishments that are not proportional to the gravity of the act committed and to the responsibility of the perpetrator (Vargas 1998).

Another example is the Right to Strike, which is recognized in Costa Rican law, but the maintenance of essential services must be ensured of the community. It is thus perceived as any standard, it can imply a concrete objective of Reasonability.

In Europe, if you find an explicit enshrinement in the European Convention on Human Rights and Fundamental Freedoms (2010) in its Articles 8, 9, 10 and 11 of the Convention:

"Article 8 Right to respect for private and family life, where there can be no interference by public authority in the exercise of this right except insofar as such interference is provided for by law and constitutes a measure which, in a democratic society, is necessary for national security, public security. Art 9 Freedom of thought, conscience and religion, whose convictions may not be subject to any restrictions other than those provided for by law and which constitute necessary measures in a democratic society Art 10 Freedom of expression, where the exercise of these freedoms, which entails duties and responsibilities, may be subject to certain formalities, conditions, restrictions or sanctions, provided for by law, which constitute necessary measures, in a democratic society. Art 11 Freedom of assembly and association: the exercise of these rights may not be subject to any restrictions other than those provided for by law and which constitute necessary measures, in a democratic society, for national security, public safety.

In turn, the European Court of Human Rights, in its jurisprudence, has frequently operated with the Principle for the Control of Interventions by Member States in the Protection of Fundamental Rights and Freedoms recognized by the Convention. At the same time, the Strasbourg Court has stated that Member States must respect the requirements of proportionality or reasonableness.

It has an importance within the European Community, or the Council of Europe, in the European Constitution (2004), in the Charter of Fundamental Rights (2000), Constitutional Treaty of the Union (2004), Treaty of Lisbon (2004), and in the German, Spanish, Austrian, Swiss, French, Italian and British public law, among others.

F. Characteristics of Legal Reasonability

To begin with, it is appropriate to recognize that the application of the principle of reasonableness cannot be fully rational if it is not applied to fundamental rights.

Similarly, it is applied for a Constitutional Control where Reasonability is carried out by applying a series of rules or judgments to the Laws that are submitted to its rigour, in general, in a contentious case.

Continental jurisprudence makes three judgments based on the system of the three sub principles. That the control of Reasonability, to enjoy a scientific rigor, must be systematically organized in a series of tests that serve to determine the Constitutional validity of the content of a norm. In accordance with

With the system of the three sub principles, it is necessary to analyze the Reasonability or Proportionality of a measure by applying judgments in a staggered and exclusive manner.

The so-called Principle that has been repeatedly mentioned in this research, actually constitutes a system that many authors have called "Reasonability Test" (Fernandez 2008).

"This protocol is applied in phases, so that if the examination of a first phase is unsatisfactory, it is unnecessary to continue with the study of the rest of the aspects, although, in some cases, for greater force of the failure can be deepened. It is a useful "protocol" to force the judge to explain why a certain measure is considered disproportionate. Part of this exercise involves weighing the degree of danger of the sanctioned conduct with respect to the protected good" (Res. No. 2011013393 Constitutional Chamber of the Supreme Court of Justice. San José).

The idea is to propose a methodology for applying this principle that will be useful for presenting the arguments used to classify something as reasonable or not6.

In this way, it operates as a real test through which a control is carried out on the normative acts in order to elucidate whether or not they are in conformity with the

---

[6] Res. N° 2011013393 Constitutional Chamber of the Supreme Court of Justice. San José, at fourteen hours and thirty minutes of October 5, 2011

Constitution, and as a tool to provide reasons for what has been decided (Sapag 2008).

"The German doctrine made a contribution to the issue of 'reasonableness by identifying its components: legitimacy, suitability, necessity, and proportionality in the strict sense. Legitimacy refers to the fact that the objective sought by the challenged act or provision must not be legally prohibited; suitability indicates that the state measure in question must be suitable for effectively achieving the objective sought; necessity means that, among several measures that are equally suitable for achieving that objective, it must choose the one that affects the individual's legal sphere as little as possible; and proportionality in the strict sense provides that the norm must be suitable and necessary and must not be out of proportion to the objective" [Sala Constitucional de Costa Rica Voto Número 3933-98].

Thus, there are three sub-principles that derive from the maximum of Reasonability: the sub-principle of suitability or adequacy, the sub-principle of necessity or indispensability, and the sub-principle of proportionality (in the strict sense if the principle of proportionality is used in Europe).

In sentence number 2008-05179 at eleven hours on April 4, two thousand eight, of the Constitutional Chamber in San José, it ratifies the above when it states that the components of Reasonability or Proportionality are Necessity, suitability, and proportionality in the strict sense. Thus, a limiting or declaratory act of Rights is Reasonable when it meets a triple condition: it is necessary, suitable and proportional.

In the sentence number 08858-98, of the sixteen hours and thirty three minutes of December 15, 1998, it was the object of a recent development, resolution in which the guidelines for its analysis were indicated, both of the administrative acts and of the norms of general character:

"Thus, an act limiting rights is reasonable when it meets a triple condition: it is **necessary, appropriate** *and* **proportional***. The* **need for** *a measure refers directly to the existence of a factual basis that makes it necessary to protect some good or set of goods of the community - or of a certain group - by adopting a differentiation measure. In other words, if such action is not taken, important public interests will be harmed. If the limitation is not necessary, it cannot be considered reasonable, and therefore constitutionally valid. The suitability of the measure depends on a judgment as to whether or not the type of restriction to be adopted complies with the purpose of satisfying the need detected. The inappropriateness of the measure would indicate that there may be other mechanisms that could better solve the existing need, some of which could fulfill the proposed purpose without restricting the enjoyment of the right in question. In turn, proportionality refers to a judgment of necessary comparison between the purpose of the act and the type of restriction that is imposed or intended to be imposed, so that the limitation is not significantly greater than the benefit it is intended to obtain for the benefit of the community. Of the last two elements, it could be said*

that the first is based on a qualitative judgment, while the second is based on a

quantitative comparison of the objects analyzed

Even so, Robert (1993) argues that the maxim of Proportionality is not so much a Principle but rather a concept that regulates the application of all Principles in the Legal System when they conflict, and that it encompasses three rules: adequacy, necessity and proportionality in the strict sense (Sapag 2008).

There are three aspects according to which the proportion between the Principle protected by the arbitrated means and the Principle protected by the desired end is compared. In this way, the constitutionality of the acts of government is controlled on the basis of an analysis between the measure and the intended purpose or, in other words, between the costs and the benefits of a measure.

But it is also a criterion that allows us to analyze the constitutionality of fundamental rights. According to the Spanish Constitutional Court, it must be asked whether a Fundamental Rights intervention meets the requirements of the sub principles of suitability, necessity and proportionality (in the strict sense) would then be Constitutional; in the terms of the sentence:

"if such a measure is likely to achieve the proposed objective of
guaranteeing public order without danger to persons and property; if,
in addition, it is necessary in the sense that no other more moderate
measure exists for the achievement of such an objective with equal

---

[7] Ruling number 08858-98, of 16:33 hours of December 15, 1998, Constitutional Chamber of Costa Rica.

effectiveness and, finally, whether it is proportionate, that is to say,
weighted or balanced because more benefits or advantages for the
general interest are derived from it than harm to other goods or values
in conflict" (Alexy 2007).

These sub-principles are applied in a successive and staggered manner, so that if one of them is not crossed, the rule must be declared unconstitutional (Sapag 2008).

The fact that these rules are derived does not take away their character of Principle since they are tests, or judgments of verification of the Reasonability or Proportionality of a norm. In fact, if what is sought is the highest possible degree of Proportionality or Reasonability, and to detect the unreasonableness of a standard, some specific judgments are indispensable. These judgments, or rules, are guidelines that give a certain degree of objectivity and determination to the Principle of Reasonability.

Bernal pulido (2003) points out that *"the sub principles of proportionality have the character of rules".*

In effect, in Judgment 253/1993 of November 29, 1993 of the Spanish Constitutional Court, the following was expressed with respect to this situation:

"The test of reasonableness also depends on the type of test to be
verified and, in this regard, the criterion required will be the existence
of an objective parameter that beyond all reasonable doubt allows to
establish unequivocally what has to be assessed as correct answers
to certain

issues. In general, the test type exams allow in greater measure the existence of these objective parameters and the correlative unequivocal determination of the correct answers".

The principle of proportionality and the requirements of sub-principles express a set of conditions of rationality that all state measures must comply with, and which also have a link to the content of political deliberation, thus becoming a constitutional limit to the actions of the legislature, which it must respect (Sánchez 2007).

It imposes a fine examination, often profound and subtle, of the relationship between a certain public interest or another principle, not only protected but constitutionally required, which would affect a Fundamental Right and its effectiveness, and it raises arguments that force us to go beyond the undoubted constitutional legitimacy of the latter.

E.1 Need

The judgment or sub-principle of necessity (or indispensability as it is also known) examines the degree of proportionality of the measure with respect to other equally effective or even more effective measures.

The Constitutional Chamber of Costa Rica reiterates this when it says that necessity means that among several measures equally suitable for achieving such an objective, the competent authority must choose the one that affects the person's legal sphere as little as possible (Constitutional Chamber Ruling number 03933-98, of the nine hours fifty-nine minutes of the twelfth day of June, nineteen hundred and ninety-eight).

The judgment of necessity is nothing other than a quality control of the rules governing fundamental rights. It is a requirement of the Principle of Reasonability that the standard adopted to achieve the required purpose is the best one, and not only the effective or adequate one (Sapag 2008).

To this end, it is necessary to consider the circumstances of the measure: time, manner and place; in this sense, the reasonable standard will be, among other things, the one that is most economical, the one that achieves the purpose in the shortest time possible, the one that entails the least costs and efforts for the community, the one that regulates the least number of assumptions of fact and subjects reached, etc.

The legislative act must be appropriate for the realization of the ends that underlie it; it must be necessary, it must impose the least amount of restrictions to Fundamental Rights, which means that the means employed by the legislator must be adequate and necessary to achieve the proposed objective and, it is necessary, when the legislator could not have chosen another means, equally efficient, but which does not limit or make less sensitive the Fundamental Right (Constitutional Chamber of the Supreme Court of Justice of San José, at ten hours thirty-one minutes of May twenty-seventh, two thousand and eleven. Res. 20110- 6805).

Then, the legislative measure that restricts a Fundamental Right must be the strictly indispensable one to satisfy the end that those are trying to oppose because: it is the least burdensome for the affected Right, among diverse options equally suitable to achieve the mentioned end or there are no options to satisfy the desired end or those available affect the intervened law to a greater extent. If one of the above-mentioned assumptions is not met, the measure in question will be illegitimate because it would interfere with a Fundamental Right that is not strictly necessary (Sánchez 2007).

The study to establish whether or not a certain restrictive measure of Fundamental Rights is necessary requires an analysis of the efficiency of its alternatives, in accordance with the applicable sciences and techniques. Although this task may be infinite, since a large number of options of the former can be proposed, a more or less extensive catalog of them must undoubtedly be exposed in the process, depending on the circumstances (Sapag 2008).

The need for a measure directly refers to the existence of a factual basis that makes it necessary to protect some good or set of goods of the community or a certain group by adopting a differentiation measure. In other words, if such action is not taken, important public interests will be harmed. If the limitation is not necessary, it cannot be considered reasonable, and therefore constitutionally valid (Res. No. 2008-05179 constitutional chamber of the supreme court of justice. San José, at eleven hours on April 4, 2008).

In this regard, it is important to note Decision No. 90, 145 of the Second Chamber of the German Federal Constitutional Court, issued on March 9, 1994, which indicated the following:

"In accordance with this principle of reasonableness, the law restricting a fundamental right must be adequate and necessary to achieve the desired end. A law is adequate, (or suitable) when with its help the desired result can be achieved; it is necessary, when the legislator could not have chosen another equally effective means that does not restrict or limit the fundamental right to a lesser extent. Additionally, in order to fully weigh the seriousness of the intervention against the weight, as well as the depth of the grounds that justify it, the limits of enforceability for the addressees of the prohibition must be taken into account. The measures, therefore, must not be overly burdensome (prohibition of overreach or duty of proportionality in the strict sense).

Many legislative decisions have the defect of legitimately affecting a Fundamental *ius* rule, especially when a Constitutional interest is invoked to justify it; but a deeper and more detailed analysis of them results in the unnecessary violation of a Constitutional guaranteed legal position to the governed, since there are alternative decisions that cease to affect one or several Fundamental Rights and that obtain better results for the purpose they pursue or bring about both consequences (Sánchez 2007).

Cianciardo (2004) argues that it is a mistake for judges to exempt themselves from this control, and summarizes his position in six arguments:

First, the Rights are considered operational and it is up to the judges to make them as operational as possible.

Secondly, public bodies play an active advocacy role, so judges are also called upon to do so.

Thirdly, the Principle of Reasonability can be turned into a means to end up justifying strong interference with Fundamental Rights.

Fourthly, the same idea of principle means that they must be optimized, and then there is no limit to their application when they are called upon to maximize.

Fifthly, contemporary legal theory recognizes that a mechanical application of the law is impossible and that judges cannot escape assessment.

Finally, the judgment of necessity must be harmonized with that of self-containment or the declaration of unconstitutionality as the last ratio of the legal system.

E.2 Suitability

The judgment or sub-principle of adequacy (or suitability) is to detect the purpose of the measure and then determine whether it is constitutionally and socially relevant. Once the end has been detected, it must be analyzed whether the means is suitable to achieve it. This is a judgment of effectiveness, that is, the means to achieve in some way the proposed end (Sapag 2008).

A rule that establishes means that are not capable of achieving the desired end must be declared unconstitutional for unreasonableness (Sapag 2008).

It should be noted that suitability does not examine the most effective measure to achieve the goal, but rather that it is solvent to achieve the purpose that is considered imperative.

It will mean that a measure is valid to reach a previously proposed objective (Lépiz 2009).

It is important to make a judgment as to whether or not the type of restriction to be adopted complies with the purpose of satisfying the need detected. The adequacy of the measure would indicate that there may be other mechanisms that better solve the existing need, some of them may meet the proposed purpose without restricting the enjoyment of the right in question (Res. No. 2008-05179 constitutional chamber of the supreme court of justice. San José, at eleven hours of April 4, 2008).

This suitability expresses the requirement that any limitation to a right (development of a right) must be adequate in relation to a constitutionally legitimate purpose (from Assisi 2006).

It examines the effectiveness of the means adopted in relation to the purpose pursued by the standard (Sapag 2008).

Suitability indicates that the state measure in question must be suitable to effectively achieve the intended objective (Constitutional Chamber Ruling number 03933-98, of the nine hours and fifty-nine minutes of the twelfth day of June of nineteen hundred and ninety-eight).

It must be analyzed at the time and circumstances of the application of the standard. So if it was inadequate at the time of its sanction, but is adequate later, it is Reasonable. It must also be analyzed in the abstract, if in general the means do not achieve the purpose, the norm is inadequate. In both cases, unconstitutionality must be declared (Sapag 2008).

The judgement will be technical as the adequacy of the measure must be scientifically proven. In case of doubt, in general, one will be in favor of constitutionality, since the proof usually falls on the person alleging unconstitutionality. It is sufficient that the norm reaches in some way, even partially, the purpose since what is judged here is the effectiveness and not the efficiency that is the object of the judgment of necessity (Sapag 2008).

E.3 Proportionality

This sub-principle is a weighting between the Principles at stake; it requires, that the measure maintains a "Reasonable Relationship" with the purpose: it examines the cost-benefit ratio of the measure with respect to its purpose, that is, between what is obtained by the measure and what is prevented by it (Sapag 2008).

The principle of proportionality (also known as weighting) expresses the need for any appropriate and necessary limitation of a right (development of a Law) pass the test of the advantages and the sacrifices (of Assisi 2006).

More than a weighting between two conflicting principles, it means a comparison of the costs and benefits of the standard: it is advocated that if the costs exceed the benefits, the standard should be declared unconstitutional (Sapag 2008).

The nature of the measure and the relevance of the purpose must be evaluated, which will imply, in some way, an assessment by the judges that must be sufficiently founded (Sapag 2008).

But the injury to Fundamental Rights derived from the measure taken cannot be substantially greater than the benefit that the purpose would bring (Lépiz 2009).

For its part, proportionality refers to a judgment of necessary comparison between the purpose pursued by the act and the type of restriction that is imposed or intended to be imposed, so that the limitation is not of a markedly higher entity than the benefit it is intended to obtain for the benefit of the community. Of the last two elements, it could be said that the first is based on a qualitative judgment, while the second is based on a quantitative comparison of the two objects analyzed.8

The *balancing test* applied in American law to solve fundamental rights problems consists of balancing the regulated law

---

[8] File: 08-003901-0007-CO Res. No. 2008-05179 constitutional chamber of the supreme court of justice. San Jose, at eleven hours of April 4, two thousand eight

or affected by the right that seeks to protect the purpose of the measure. A similar system is applied in continental law with the weighting or conflict rule. This is not what should be sought through the judgment of proportionality; the idea of prioritizing rights, whether abstract or concrete, must be excluded (Sapag 2008).

Rather, it is intended that, through this judgment, the means are quantified and qualified in some way with respect to the ends to be achieved in order to glimpse the proportion that should exist between the costs and the benefits and, thus, provide reasons for it.

The benefits must always outweigh the costs, otherwise the standard would be meaningless. A quantitative analysis should not be carried out, but also one of economic cost, subjects reached and subjects benefited, prolongation of the measure in time and space, etc. (Sapag 2008).

It provides that, apart from the requirement that the norm be suitable and necessary, what it orders must not be out of proportion to the intended objective, in other words, not "enforceable" on the individual (Constitutional Chamber Ruling number 03933-98, of nine hours fifty-nine minutes of June 12, 1998).

The appeal to Reasonability which consists of the equality trial refers to an effort to rationally justify the decision and contains a conflict between Principles and partial factual inequalities that postulate contradictory tendencies, which may allege in its favor one of the sub principles that make up equality, and there will always be a reason for it (Fernandez 2008).

CONCLUSIONS

In effect, the principle of reasonableness implies that the State may limit or restrict the abusive exercise of the right, but it must do so in such a way that the legal norm is adapted in all its elements as the motive and the purpose it pursues, with the objective sense contemplated in the Constitution.

This means that there must be proportionality between the legal rule adopted and the end it pursues, referring to the imperative need for the law to satisfy the legal common sense of the community, expressed in the values enshrined in the Constitution itself.9

Costa Rican constitutional jurisprudence has been clear and responsive in considering that the principle of reasonableness constitutes a parameter of constitutionality in the following terms:

"The law of the Constitution, composed of the norms and principles of the Constitution and of international law, and particularly those of its human rights instruments, as the primary foundations of any positive legal order, transmit to it its own logical structure and axiological meaning, based on values that even precede the legislative texts themselves, which are in turn the source of any normative system proper to a society organized under the concepts of the rule of law, the constitutional regime, democracy, and freedom, so that any norm or act that violates those values or

---

9 Judgment number 1420-91, of 9:00 am on June 24, 1991 Constitutional Chamber of Costa Rica.

The principle of the right to freedom of thought, conscience, and religion, which is a principle of the right to freedom of thought, conscience, and religion, is a principle of the right to freedom of thought, conscience, and religion, which is a principle of the right to freedom of thought, conscience, and religion.

---

[10] Judgment number 3495-92, of 14:30 hours of November 19, 1992 Constitutional Chamber of Costa Rica

BIBLIOGRAPHY

Alexy R. (2007) The Weight Formula. Department of Publications, Universidad Externado de Colombia.

Alexy R. (2007) Fundamental Rights Theory. 2nd Edition. Editorial Centro de Estudios Políticos y Constitucionales. Spain.

Barnes J. (1994) Introduction to the Principle of Proportionality in Comparative and Community Law. Journal of Public Administration. Spain.

Bazán J. and Madrid (1991) Rationality and Reasonability in Law. Chilean Law Magazine V 18 N° Madrid, Spain.

Bidart campos G. (2000), Tratado elemental de derecho constitucional argentino, buenos aires, edit, ii-a.

Bobbio N. (1994) General Theory of Law. Reprint of the second edition. Editorial Temis S.A. Santa Fé Bogotá Colombia.

Cianciardo J. (2003) Principles and Rules: An approach from the criteria of distinction. Boletín Mexicano de Derecho Comparado, No. 108.

Cianciardo J. (2005) Del Debido Proceso Sustantivo al moderno juicio de proporcionalidad. Dikalon N 14. Colombia.

Dromi J. (1980) Subjective Law and Public Liability. Editorial TEMIS Bogotá Colombia.

Fernández Nieto J. (2008) Principle of Proportionality and Fundamental Rights: A perspective from the common European public law. Editorial DYKINSON Madrid. Spain.

González Solano G. (1996) La rationalidad Jurídica de las sentencias de la CIDH. Thesis for the degree of Licenciatura. University of Costa Rica. San José, Costa Rica.

Haba E. P. and Barth J. F. (2004) Los Principios Generales del Derecho Editorial Investigaciones Jurídicas. San José Costa Rica.

Hauriou A. (1979). Constitutional Law and Political Institutions. Editorial Ariel, Barcelona, Spain.

Lépiz O. (2009) The Strict Judgment of Reasonability. Thesis Graduate studies University of Costa Rica.

Linares J. (2002) Reasonability of the Laws. Due process as an unnamed guarantee in constitutionality. 2 edition Buenos Aires Argentina.

Mans Puigarnau J. (1978) Lógica para Juristas Editorial Bosch S.A. does not indicate edition. Spain.

Pereira Sáez C. (2004) Una Contribución al Estudio del Empleo del Principio de Proporcionalidad en la Jurisprudencia Reciente del Tribunal Constitucional. I Anuario da Facultade de Dereito da Universidade da Coruña REV AD N° 08, España.

Perelman C. (1984) Le raisonnable et le déraisonnable en droit. Beyond legal positivism. Libraire generale des Droit et de Jurisprudence. París Francia.

Sánchez Delgado D. (2003) El Principio de Razonabilidad: Origen, Desarrollo y Utilización en la Doctrina y la Jurisprudencia Costarricense. Thesis for the Master's Degree in Constitutional Law. National State Distance University. Costa Rica.

Sapag Mariano A. (2008) The Principle of Proportionality and Reasonability as a Constitutional Limit of the State: A Comparative Study. Di Kaion No. 17 Universidad de la Sabana. Colombia.

Vargas 1998Sánchez Gil, R. (2007) El Principio de Proporcionalidad Instituto de Investigaciones jurídicas. Mexico.

Vargas Montero A. (1998) Los Principios de la Razonabilidad y la Proporcionalidad dentro del Proceso Penal. Thesis from the University of Costa Rica.

Vargas Sánchez Gil, R. (2007) El Principio de Proporcionalidad Instituto de Investigaciones jurídicas. Mexico.

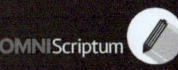